LAURIE
HALSE
ANDERSON

LAURIE HALSE ANDERSON

KRISTI LEW

ROSEN
PUBLISHING®

New York

Published in 2014 by The Rosen Publishing Group, Inc.
29 East 21st Street, New York, NY 10010

First Edition

Library of Congress Cataloging-in-Publication Data

Lew, Kristi.
Laurie Halse Anderson/Kristi Lew.—First edition.
    pages cm.—(All About the Author)
Includes bibliographical references and index.
ISBN 978-1-4777-1764-6 (library binding)
1. Anderson, Laurie Halse—Juvenile literature. 2. Authors, American—20th century—Biography—Juvenile literature.
I. Title.
PS3551.N374443Z75 2013
813'.54—dc23
[B]

2013011362

Manufactured in the United States of America

CPSIA Compliance Information: Batch #W14YA: For further information, contact Rosen Publishing, New York, New York, at 1-800-237-9932.

CONTENTS

INTRODUCTION 6

CHAPTER ONE   FAMILY LIFE..................10

CHAPTER TWO   FROM NEWSPAPERS TO NOVELS.....22

CHAPTER THREE   GIVING TEENS A VOICE............31

CHAPTER FOUR   BRINGING THE PAST ALIVE..........44

CHAPTER FIVE   BOOKS FOR YOUNG READERS...........57

CHAPTER SIX   LIVING AND LOVING THE
                 LITERARY LIFE.....................66

FACT SHEET ON
LAURIE HALSE ANDERSON...............79

FACT SHEET ON
LAURIE HALSE ANDERSON'S WORK 81

CRITICAL REVIEWS..................89

TIMELINE.......................93

GLOSSARY....................95

FOR MORE INFORMATION......98

FOR FURTHER READING...102

BIBLIOGRAPHY....105

INDEX...108

Laurie Halse Anderson is a best-selling author of realistic and historical fiction for young adults and children. Two of her books, *Speak* and *Chains*, have been nominated for the National Book Award, which honors the best of the best in American literature. Anderson was also the recipient of the 2008 ALAN Award and the 2009 Margaret A. Edwards Award for "significant and lasting achievement in young adult literature."

For Anderson, who never intended to become a writer, these awards may be gratifying, but her legions of fans do not care about accolades. They care about the books that she produces and how those books make them feel. According to a getting-to-know-you questionnaire on Simon & Schuster's Web site, the comment Anderson hears most from her readers is, "Thanks for telling the truth." Her commitment to doing so certainly comes though in her work.

Anderson's ability to get inside the heads of teens who are struggling did not come to her easily, but she rarely dwells on her past because what really matters, she says, is how you respond to the challenges that life throws at you. "The emotional scars I accumulated as a teenager did not bind me or turn my heart rigid. Why not? I was

Best-selling author Laurie Halse Anderson is passionate about her work and the way her stories affect her readers.

saved by Story," she told the audience during her acceptance speech for the Edwards Award.

Even from a young age, Anderson was surrounded by "story." She has said in many interviews that her father, a minister, was a gifted storyteller. She told Reading Rockets, a multimedia project developed by reading experts to help educators and parents support struggling readers, that her father told the best stories when he thought she was sleeping. At night, she would creep to the top of the staircase and listen. These late-night listening sessions are likely when she developed her innate sense of pacing, hooks, and dialogue that make her novels so compelling. "The stories I heard around the campfire and when I was hiding on the stairs showed me where I came from," she said in her Edwards Award speech. "The books in my high school and public libraries showed me where I could go."

Anderson's ability to tell a good story also comes through in her historical fiction, which she prefers to call "historical thrillers." In these books, Anderson skillfully weaves the true story of the history of the United States with the fictional stories of young people in peril. Her love of history and historical research are quite evident in these gripping stories. "Learning about the events and people that shaped our country never feels like work; it's fun, a giant puzzle that I like solving," she told Julie Prince in an interview for *Teacher Librarian.*

Anderson is still hard at work immersing herself in Story. According to her Web site, Mad

Woman in the Forest, her plan is to alternate writing young adult fiction and historical thrillers for the next decade. She also says that she has a few picture book ideas up her sleeve and is toying with the idea of writing a book on the writing process. She has come a long way from the woman who avoided English classes in college because she hated to analyze books, a practice, she told Patricia Newman in an interview for *California Kids!*, that made becoming an author much more difficult than it needed to be. Her many adoring fans are thankful for her persistence.

ONE

FAMILY LIFE

Laurie Beth Halse was born on October 23, 1961, in Potsdam, New York, to Frank and Joyce Holcomb Halse. She has one sibling, a younger sister named Lisa. In her biography on her Web site, Anderson says that if she could wish for anything in the world, she would ask for world peace. But if she cannot have that, she would settle for people pronouncing her maiden name correctly. "Halse" rhymes with the word "waltz."

CHILDHOOD

When she was in the first grade, Laurie's family moved from Potsdam to Syracuse, New York, where her father became a chaplain at Syracuse University. In an interview with Reading Rockets, Anderson reveals that as a child, she struggled to learn to read and had a speech impediment. When she finally got the hang of reading, however, she read voraciously. As

aurie, on her third birthday, enjoys cake and presents in her Potsdam, New ork, home.

a young reader, she especially enjoyed historical fiction. As a teenager, she was more attracted to the science fiction and fantasy genres.

According to the acknowledgments in *Wintergirls*, Anderson wasn't the best student, spending much of her time daydreaming in the back row. She told Reading Rockets that she did not like English class because she was not a very good speller and she did not feel that she had a good grasp of grammar. She credits her second-grade teacher, Mrs. Sheedy-Shea, with introducing her to haiku. Laurie especially enjoyed writing this form of poetry because the poems were short and she could pick only words she knew how to spell. Although she rarely publishes any of her poetry, Anderson still enjoys writing haiku for personal pleasure.

Her father, Reverend Frank Halse, a Methodist minister, had a hand in shaping Laurie's love for poetry. As a child, she remembers him writing and rewriting poems: choosing words, discarding them, and choosing different ones as he made the imagery in his poems better and better. She told Reading Rockets that her father influenced her love of story, too. Reverend Halse was very interested in words and language. He spoke often about the roots of words in different languages. His influence is clear as Laurie eventually went on to get a college degree in linguistics, which is the study of language and how it is organized and structured.

Although neither of Anderson's parents actively discouraged her from becoming a writer, her mother, Joyce Holcomb Halse, would have preferred that her daughter chose a more stable career, such as nursing. As a child, Laurie did entertain the idea of becoming a doctor. However, she says in her biography on the Scholastic Web site that her high school chemistry teacher would likely have found that idea laughable.

Laurie's mother did encourage her daughter's love of reading, however. Anderson told Reading Rockets that when she was a little girl and her mother found her reading instead of cleaning her room like she was told, her mother never yelled. She

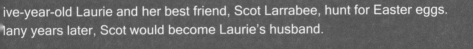

ive-year-old Laurie and her best friend, Scot Larrabee, hunt for Easter eggs.
lany years later, Scot would become Laurie's husband.

13

just told Laurie to finish the chapter and then clean up her room. As a result, Anderson says, she rarely had a clean bedroom.

"My elementary school years in Syracuse were idyllic," she said in her acceptance speech for the 2009 Margaret A. Edwards Award. "I was shy, except when it came to games of pretend or putting on plays. Then I turned into Miss Bossy-Pants, which was tolerated, barely, because I was good at making things up."

LIFE AT SCHOOL

This all changed when Anderson was thirteen and her father had a falling out with the church. All of a sudden, her idyllic world was turned upside down. Her father left the ministry and fell into a deep depression. The house the Halses lived in belonged to the church, too, so they were forced to move from the neighborhood that Laurie had grown to love. In addition, with her father out of a job, her mother was required to work long, hard hours to support the family. "I was lost," Anderson says of those years.

Though her parents could not afford private school, Anderson received a scholarship to Manlius Pebble Hill

School, a college prepa-
ratory academy in DeWitt,
New York, for her eighth-
grade year. She credits
one of Manlius Pebble
Hill's English teachers,
David Edwards, with

aurie Halse (indicated by a red circle)
oses with her eighth grade classmates
t Manlius Pebble Hill School. She is
lso seen at the right during the same
cademic year.

helping her build a foundation for her future writing life by introducing her to Greek mythology. In her acknowledgments for *Wintergirls*, she seems to have her doubts that Edwards realized that she really was paying attention in his class. She believes that she may have been a very frustrating student for him and says she regrets that he died before he could hold one of her published books.

According to Anderson's keynote speech for the 2004 Arizona English Teacher's Association State Convention, which was reprinted in the *ALAN Review*, Anderson did not enjoy her high school years very much. In fact, she says her ninth-grade year was "torture." Because of these experiences, and her fascination with languages and world cultures, Laurie decided to spend her senior year abroad. As an American Field Service (now AFS-USA) exchange student, she spent her senior year living on a pig farm and going to school in Denmark. Anderson told fellow children's book author Debbi Michiko Florence that on the pig farm, she learned to do many of the things a farmer needs to do, such as removing rocks from a field, feeding livestock, and, of course, scooping manure. She learned how to butcher ducks and pigs, too. "I also grew up and had the time of my life," she said.

On her return to the United States, Anderson went to work in a clothing store. The minimum-wage

Georgetown University, located in Washington, D.C., is acclaimed for encouraging the study of foreign languages and cultures. Anderson graduated from Georgetown with a degree in language and linguistics in 1984.

salary that she was paid convinced her to go to college. She told Debbi Michiko Florence that her family had always had the expectation that she would go to college, but she did not consider herself a very good student and was not sure that she would make it through. As a result, she attended Onondaga Community College in Syracuse, New York, and received her two-year associate's degree before making the commitment to go to a four-year university. While at the community college, she worked on a dairy farm, milking cows. In 1981, she transferred to Georgetown University in Washington, D.C. She graduated from Georgetown in 1984 with a bachelor's degree in language and linguistics.

NO PROM ON A PIG FARM

While on tour for her book *Prom*, Anderson was often asked about her senior prom. In an interview with Yahoo! Voices, she revealed that she did not attend her senior prom. She was in Denmark living on a pig farm at the time. Nevertheless, she did go to a few proms when she was a sophomore and junior in high school. Furthermore, before she wrote *Prom*, all four of her children had gone to their proms and she had been involved in all of their planning. She used these experiences to make the book more realistic.

MARRIAGE AND FAMILY

Laurie married Greg Anderson in 1983 and gave birth to their oldest daughter, Stephanie Holcomb, in 1985. Another daughter, Meredith Lauren, followed in 1987. Laurie and Greg divorced in 2002 but remain friends. In fact, Anderson still relies on Greg to proofread her manuscripts to look for grammatical errors. Greg Anderson later married Dr. Susan J. Kressley, a pediatrician. According to her biography on the Scholastic Web site, Laurie considers Susan to be a good friend and an "awesome stepmom." In the acknowledgments for *Wintergirls*, she also credits Dr. Kressley for encouraging her to tackle the subject of eating disorders and for reading early drafts of the manuscript and providing feedback.

In 2004, Anderson married her childhood sweetheart, Scot Larrabee, and became stepmom to Jessica and Christian. The children have all left home now, but Anderson and Larrabee still live in Mexico, New York, close to Lake Ontario. Their family also includes a brood of chickens and a German shepherd named Kezzie that, Anderson told Kathleen Horning in an interview for the *School Library Journal*, "excels at barking at chipmunks and laying on my feet."

When she's not writing, Anderson enjoys gardening, hiking, and training for marathons. On her blog,

When she is not writing, Anderson enjoys training for and running marathons with her husband, Scot.

she says that she is not the fastest runner. "When God was handing out speed, I was in the library reading," she says. Nonetheless, she seems to enjoy the marathons and the training. After running her first marathon in November 2011, she wrote on her blog that running a marathon is very much like writing a book—scary and exhilarating at the same time. With twenty-eight books published to date and several more in the works, Anderson is certainly no stranger to the discipline and determination it takes to run a marathon—or to write a novel.

CHAPTER TWO

FROM NEWSPAPERS TO NOVELS

Her early teachers may have thought the idea of Anderson becoming a doctor was laughable, but they did not think she would become a writer either, she told Reading Rockets. Yet, she was interested in writing and after finishing her college degree, she landed a job as a reporter for the *Philadelphia Inquirer.* In her keynote address to the 2004 Arizona English Teacher's Association State Convention, reprinted in the *ALAN Review*, Anderson says the experience helped her because she had "wonderful editors who taught me how to write (once they finished throwing dictionaries at my head)."

BECOMING A YOUNG ADULT AUTHOR

According to an interview with Debbi Michiko Florence, Anderson became interested in writing fiction for children when her own children began to read. At that time, she set a goal of having a children's book published five years after her youngest child entered first grade. Four years later, in 1996, her first picture book, *Ndito Runs*, was published. She had made her goal—with one year to spare.

Like most authors, Anderson found the road to publication a bumpy one. On her blog, she reveals that she made a lot of mistakes as a beginning writer. "I sent out first drafts [and] I collected hundreds of well-deserved rejection letters," she says. However, she learned from those rejection letters and went on to publish another picture book, *Turkey Pox*, and several chapter books for young readers.

After that, she turned her sights on writing historical fiction for middle grade students. She found that, despite her initial success in picture and chapter books, her days of being rejected were not over. *Fever 1793*, her first historical novel, was rejected thirteen times. While she was still struggling to revise that book, the idea for her first young adult novel, *Speak*, came to her in a dream. The idea

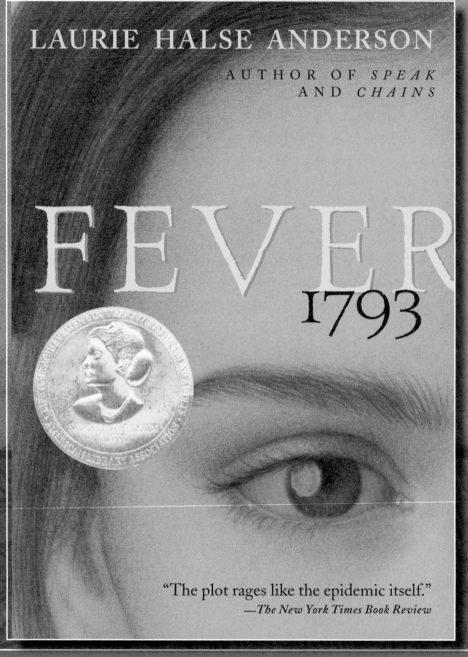

LAURIE HALSE ANDERSON

AUTHOR OF *SPEAK*
AND *CHAINS*

FEVER
1793

"The plot rages like the epidemic itself."
—*The New York Times Book Review*

Published in 2000, *Fever 1793* was Anderson's first historical thriller. In the following year, the American Library Association chose it as one of the 2001 Best Books for Young Adults.

was so compelling that Anderson would put *Fever 1793* aside for a year while she wrote the young adult novel. In a blog post for *The Debutante Ball*, Anderson wrote, "After writing *Speak*, I returned to *Fever 1793* and was able to see all of the weaknesses of the story." So she set about revising it. Her hard work and determination paid off. The next time she sent *Fever 1793* to an editor, she got a phone call saying they would like to publish it.

In her acceptance speech for her 2009 Margaret A. Edwards Award, Anderson credits her ability to write such wrenching, realistic stories for teens to her troubled teenage years. Although she did not experience the same situations that she has crafted

A TATTOO OF A STORYTELLER

Anderson is passionate about story. So passionate, in fact, a picture on Sarah Stormie Campbell's blog, *Card Catalog of Creativity*, shows that she has the word "Hwæt" tattooed on the inside of her right wrist. Hwæt is the first word of the Old English epic poem *Beowulf*. Literally translated, the word means "what," but in the days of oral storytelling, the word had a slightly different meaning. When the storyteller was about to begin, he or she used the word "Hwæt" to mean "Listen to this!" or "Hear me!"

for her characters, she certainly felt some of the same emotions she ascribes to them. She went on to explain that she handled those painful emotions by taking "control and ma[king] my own choices. I certainly wasn't planning on it, but somehow I became an author."

WRITING PROCESS

Anderson says on her blog that her writing process has changed over the years, depending on how many children were living at home, whether she was married or a single mother, and how many elderly parents needed to be taken care of. One aspect appears to remain the same: Anderson is an early riser. When *Speak* was published in 1999, Anderson told *Publishers Weekly* that she got up at 4:30 AM to write in her journal before the rest of her family got up. She then got the kids off to school and settled down to write until noon. After lunch was time for research and reading. In 2012, she wrote that she wakes up at 5:00 and tries to begin writing by 6:00 AM. She is often still at it when dinnertime rolls around.

In a 2008 interview with Julie Prince for *Teacher Librarian*, she said, "I generally work seven days a week, though I try to take half-days off on the weekends and for holidays." Finding a way to balance her writing time, her family, traveling for speaking

From strengthening her gift of storytelling to supporting her love of reading, Anderson's parents, Reverend Frank Halse and Joyce Holcomb Halse, gave their daughter the foundation she needed to become a successful author.

engagements, reading, and research seems to be a common theme no matter where she is in her career.

When asked to give advice for aspiring authors, Anderson told *Teen Ink* that beginning writers need to believe in themselves. Do not listen to the nay-sayers who say you cannot write, she advised. Keep trying. She also emphasized the fact that revision is a fact of life for people who write for a living. "Real writers revise their work over and over and over," she said. "Just turn off the television and write."

WHY IS IT MAD WOMAN IN THE FOREST?

In a YouTube video titled "Why Mad Woman in the Forest?," Anderson answers while sitting outside in the woodland that surrounds her northern New York home. She says, "These woods have a lot to do with who I am and why I became a writer." She goes on to explain that she has been camping in the foothills of the Adirondack Mountains since she was three years old. As she and her best friend, Scot, who is now her husband, played among the hills, she says she pretended to be a pirate queen, a scout, and an explorer. She credits these early experiences of creating stories and allowing her imagination to run free with her development as a storyteller and, consequently, as an author. Considering her publishing schedule, it also appears that she writes like a madwoman!

REACHING OUT TO READERS

Anderson established her Web site, Mad Woman in the Forest, in 2000. However, she told *School Library Journal* that she did not do much with it in the beginning. It wasn't until *Prom* was published, around 2005, that she started to blog. "It felt like the floodgates opened," she says. When asked why she thinks so many readers reach out to her, Anderson says she believes they respond to the honesty in her writing. She doesn't sugarcoat the issues, no matter how messy and uncomfortable they might be. Now there are many ways for her to reach out to readers and for them to communicate with her, a process she really seems to enjoy.

Readers often write her to say that they identified with one of the characters in her books and that the book helped them understand something they had not understood before. Or they might say that they learned to approach a particular problem in a different way. Basically, they write to thank her. Anderson says these messages are the reason she

Growing up playing make-believe in the foothills of the Adirondack Mountains allowed Anderson to develop and strengthen her imagination from a young age.

keeps writing. They are her inspiration. She feels as if, somehow, she may be able to help.

"I just have such respect for teenagers," she told School Library Journal, "especially the teenagers right now. It's so much harder than when [I was] growing up." She also says she is impressed each time she witnesses the young people of this generation treating each other with tolerance and respect.

Although she does seem truly to enjoy communicating with readers, she does not necessarily appreciate getting e-mails asking her to do someone's homework, especially if they have not taken the time to read the book. She told School Library Journal, "It's a little frustrating to get an e-mail from an 11th-grade reader at 11 on a Sunday night requesting that I explain to this kid who's got to turn in his essay the next morning all the symbolism in whatever book."

In the interview for Teacher Librarian, Julie Prince asked Anderson how she balances sharing herself with readers and maintaining privacy. She says that growing up with a father who was a minister taught her how to interact with people while maintaining certain boundaries. Even so, she says, "for the most part it's really fun to have so many friends and friendly readers. Sharing my life and communicating through the blog builds community and I like that."

GIVING TEENS A VOICE

A nderson did not like being a teenager, and she certainly never intended to become a young adult author, she told the audience in her keynote speech for the Arizona English Teacher's Association State Convention. But that was before she woke up in the middle of the night to the sound of a girl weeping.

SPEAK

That sobbing girl turned out to be Melinda Sordino, the protagonist in her first young adult novel, *Speak*. As the book opens, Melinda is beginning her freshman year at Merryweather High. After calling the police to an out-of-hand end-of-summer party, Melinda has been rejected by her friends and has become a pariah to much of the student body. The reader soon finds out that Melinda experienced something horrible at that party. Something she cannot speak of.

THREE

FROM PAGE TO SCREEN

According to an article in the *Hollywood Reporter*, an independent film based on *Speak* premiered at the 2004 Sundance Film Festival. The movie starred Kristen Stewart, the actress who later went on to play the character Bella in the *Twilight* saga. When she acted in *Speak*, Kristen was thirteen years old, the same age as the character Melinda. The film was broadcast on the Showtime and Lifetime networks in 2005. Anderson told *Teen Ink* that she was offered the opportunity to write the script for the movie, but she turned it down because she was too busy at the time. She did get to see some of the filming, though. "I was on the set for three days," she says, "and had a cameo appearance as the lunch lady who serves Melinda mashed potatoes in the cafeteria."

A young Kristen Stewart plays the part of Melinda Sordino in the movie version of *Speak*. Melinda becomes a mute after being sexually assaulted during the summer before she enters high school.

When Anderson first heard Melinda's voice, she was in the middle of writing *Fever 1793*, but she knew she needed to put *Fever* aside until she got Melinda's story down on paper. According to Jennifer Brown in an article in *Publishers Weekly*, Anderson wrote the first draft that same night. As is her habit, however, she revised the manuscript several times before sending it out to an editor who had previously rejected one of her picture books.

Speak was published in 1999 by Farrar, Straus & Giroux. That year, it became a National Book Award finalist and Printz Honor book. It was also listed in the American Library Association's (ALA) Top Ten Best Books for Young Adults in 2000.

A tenth-anniversary edition of the book was released in 2009; it includes a heart-wrenching poem that Anderson constructed by pulling phrases from some of the tens of thousands of fan letters and e-mails she has received from readers of *Speak* over the years. Though many of the readers reaching out to Anderson are survivors of sexual assault, she said in her acceptance speech for the Edwards Award that "they also write to me about harassment, about bullying, about feeling powerless and about feeling voiceless." She titled the poem *"Listen"*.

Since its publication, *Speak* has gone on to become required reading in many high school classrooms. Experiencing the emotions the story engenders and participating in the discussions of the book that comes afterward seem to have informed and enlightened many of its readers. In an interview with *School Library Journal*, Anderson says, "I often hear from girls who write to me: 'Now I know why my mom doesn't like me to go to those kinds of parties.' Those girls just didn't get it before. They thought their moms were just being a pain in the neck." Anderson also says that she hears from male readers who say they have a better understanding of why a girl might react as Melinda did to such an experience.

CENSORSHIP AND *SPEAK*

Just before the ALA's Banned Books Week in October 2010, Wesley Scroggins, an associate professor at Missouri State University, demanded that *Speak* be taken out of the public school curriculum. He called the book "soft pornography" in an opinion piece published in the *Springfield News-Leader.*

Anderson was horrified. She took to Twitter to discuss the attempted ban. It was then, the *New York Times* reported, that Paul W. Hankins, a high school English teacher in Indiana, created the hashtag #speakloudly. Shortly thereafter, Judy Blume, one of Anderson's idols and a young adult author who has seen her share of controversy over the years, rallied behind her, calling the situation "outrageous" and promising to bring it to the attention of the National Coalition Against Censorship.

Anderson credits her readers for helping her speak out against such challenges. She told *School Library Journal* that her "readers have changed the world by declaring that rape victims have nothing to be ashamed of, but that book banners like Scroggins do." When asked if she gets tired of having to defend her work, Anderson replied, "It's time-consuming to respond to these outbreaks of censorship. I would rather be working on a new book, but we can't allow our precious intellectual freedoms to be stolen by thugs. And so, I speak. Loudly."

CATALYST

Catalyst, Anderson's second young adult novel, is set in the same high school that *Speak* is set in. Melinda makes a brief appearance in this book, too. However, unlike freshman outcast Melinda, Kate Malone, the protagonist of *Catalyst*, is an overachieving, chemistry-obsessed high school senior who is waiting desperately for her college acceptance letter from the Massachusetts Institute of Technology (MIT). While all her peers receive acceptance letters to their choice schools, Kate struggles to hold it all together as the sole caretaker of her overworked, unrealistic minister father and fourteen-year-old asthmatic brother. Then, just as Kate thought her life could not get more out of control, her nemesis, Teri Litch, and her two-year-old brother, Mikey, move into the Malone household and take over Kate's bedroom after their house is damaged in a fire.

Anderson told Debbi Michiko Florence, "I wanted to write about a teenager whose interests and passions were completely removed from mine. And I loathed chemistry in high school." Which meant, Anderson says, she had to actually learn chemistry "from the ground up" to understand Kate.

She also told Florence the story of how the title, *Catalyst*, which refers to a chemical substance that speeds up the rate of a reaction, came about. She said that she and her editor were at a conference, taking the same workshop. Anderson would write down a proposed title on a piece of paper and show it to her editor, who would shake her head. Not quite right. Her editor came up with a few possibilities, too, but Anderson did not like any of those either. At one point, her editor was called out of the room. While she was gone, Anderson thought of the perfect title—*Catalyst*—and wrote it on a separate piece of paper. Her editor came back and whispered to Anderson that she had thought of a great title—*Catalyst*. Anderson flipped over the piece of paper and showed her editor the title she had written. "We both got goose-bumps," she said. It was perfect.

PROM

Prom is probably the lightest of Anderson's young adult novels to date. The story is about high school senior Ashley Hannigan, who just wants to graduate, get out of her crazy—but loving—family home, get a job, and start her "real" life. What she does not care about is going to the prom. Her best friend, Natalia, however, is all about the prom and when a teacher steals the prom fund, Nat is heartbroken and ropes Ashley into helping her figure out what to do to save the day.

Anderson and her husband, Scot, celebrate the release of *Prom* at a bookstore in Oswego, New York. At the far left, Christian and Jessica Larrabee talk to the bookstore's owner.

In *Catalyst* and *Prom*, Anderson explores the class distinction between college-bound teens and those who don't go to college. "One of the things that really irritates me is how we, as a culture, marginalize the kids who don't go to college," she told Florence. She goes on to say that every teenager should be able to explore all of his or her options and be allowed to follow his or her passion "without being made to feel stupid or unworthy" just because that path does not lead to higher education.

TWISTED

Twisted is Anderson's first novel written from a male perspective. The video game–playing, geeky protagonist, Tyler Miller, begins his senior year of high school buffer than he has ever been before, thanks to a summer of hard labor that he was sentenced to as part of his probation for "The Foul Deed."

Just as Tyler is starting to adjust to his new status among the student body, his clueless, self-absorbed father insists that the whole family attend a party thrown by his boss. At the home of his father's boss is the boss's daughter, Bethany, Tyler's secret crush, and Tyler's most hated enemy, the boss's son. To Tyler's profound embarrassment, the goddess Bethany seems suddenly fascinated by his chiseled physique. But who is he to argue? He goes for it with heartfelt gratitude.

Then Bethany invites Tyler to a party with kids who never would have given him the time of day in the past, and Tyler is accused of a crime he did not commit. His past comes back to haunt him when everyone, including his father, is convinced that he is guilty because he has been in trouble before. In the end, Tyler must come to terms with what it means to be a man in the world today and the tough decisions that sometimes have to be made.

Anderson told *School Library Journal* that she gets messages from young men who are struggling with the same types of issues that Tyler is wrestling with. In one e-mail, a fan told her, "I don't even know why I'm writing this to you except that your book helped me make sense of a couple of things. So I guess I'm writing to say thank you." Anderson says she feels honored that teens feel they can reach out to her. This type of communication inspires her and makes her want to continue writing for this audience, she says.

WINTERGIRLS

In *Wintergirls*, Anderson once again delves into deep, dark, disturbingly realistic topics: eating disorders and cutting. The story is about two best friends, Lia and Cassie, who have decided to be the skinniest girls ever. Their dangerous contest ends up with one of them dead and the other fighting to

Many teenage girls worry about their weight. Some obsess over it. When this obsession goes to extremes, as it does with characters in *Wintergirls*, it can turn fatal.

figure out how to live. Anderson employs literary devices rarely seen in print, such as strikethrough and blank pages, to effectively establish the presence of an unreliable narrator.

Dr. Susan Kressley, Anderson's friend and the wife of her former husband, Greg, had been encouraging her to write a book about eating disorders for years. But Anderson told *School Library Journal*, "I was really reluctant to do this because I have struggled since about 12 with my own body-image issues."

In the end, Kressley won out and was instrumental in steering her toward psychiatrists who specialize in working with adolescents with eating disorders. Anderson also researched the book by reading medical journals and visiting pro-anorexia Web sites to try to understand the mind-set of the girls who frequent them.

Anderson has said that researching and writing *Wintergirls* made her more compassionate and that she came away with more love for herself. She says that even as an adult, she sometimes finds herself thinking negatively about specific body parts. She believes that to be an incredible waste of time and now tries not to be sorry about all the time she spent hating her body.

FOUR

BRINGING THE PAST ALIVE

Anderson has always loved American history. In her acceptance speech for the Edwards Award, she said that if it had not been for her painful adolescence and the appearance of Melinda Sordino in her dreams, she would most likely be writing only historical fiction.

She told Reading Rockets that she realized "children need historical stories in order to develop their own sense of morality" when her daughter, Meredith, was in middle school and went through a phase of reading fictionalized tales about the Holocaust. When Anderson asked her daughter why she was reading such dark material, Meredith replied that she was trying to figure out what she would have done if she were in the same situation as the characters in the books. At that point,

ler daughter Meredith *(sitting at the table)* helped Anderson *(right)* understand ow historical fiction informs and influences young people's lives. Anderson's aughter Stephanie stands at the left.

Anderson says, she came to believe that children in the middle grades, especially, find it easier to think about tough issues when there is a bit of a buffer between them and the reality of the story. "Historical fiction allows me to create fictional characters who participate in real-world situations," she told Nancy Hadway and Terrell Young in an interview for *Reading Today.*

CONDUCTING HISTORICAL RESEARCH

However, Anderson continued, she must balance the needs of her fictional character with the actual history of the period the book is set in. "In children's literature," she told Reading Rockets, "you can't get away with making up facts about the history." Teachers, she says, do not want to use books that present information about history that is not factual, even if the book itself is fictional.

To get her facts straight, Anderson does a lot of research. She told *Reading Today* that the overall, background research really began in 1993, when she started researching her first historical novel, *Fever 1793*. As she researched that book, she found tidbits about historical events and figures that piqued her interest. For each subsequent book, she starts her research with one of those tidbits and digs from there. She says it takes her about a year to research a particular book and approximately another year to write it. When she has finished writing, she has professional historians read the book to make sure it is as historically accurate as possible.

She says she envisions "classrooms filled with kids who have been bored to death by the dreadful way most textbooks present American history" reading her historical novels and, hopefully, enjoying history for the first time. "Storytelling is the traditional way history is passed form one generation to the next. Good storytelling brings history alive. When history fires the imagination of a reader, that child will never forget the lessons she's learned from it," she told *Reading Today.*

WHAT DOES IT TAKE TO BRING HISTORY ALIVE?

Much of the research Anderson does for her historical novels comes from primary sources, such as diaries of soldiers and advertisements or newspaper stories of the period—but not all of it. "I wrote *Forge* in a small cabin in the northern woods, heated by wood that I split and carried," Anderson noted on her blog. She also reports in an article she published in *Horn Book Magazine* that she wrote by candlelight and walked shoeless in the snow. All this in an effort to understand what a Continental army soldier would have gone through at Valley Forge in the winter of 1777. She also "cooked and tasted (and loathed) fire cake," a mixture of flour and water patted into cake form and baked in the ashes of a fire until blackened. "I tasted gunpowder," she continued. "It was almost as nasty as the fire cake."

Julie Prince asked Anderson if she had a research assistant in an interview with *Teacher Librarian*. "I can't afford a research assistant," Anderson replied. "But even if I could, I am not sure that I would hire one." She says that she often finds information while researching one book that leads her to details that make the book much more realistic. Her research sometimes leads her to ideas for other books, too. She worries that a research assistant would not recognize the type of details and ideas that resonate with her.

FEVER 1793

Fever 1793 is the story of a yellow fever outbreak in Philadelphia, Pennsylvania, in July 1793, when Philadelphia served as America's capital city. By the time the outbreak peaked in October of that year, the city had lost nearly half of its residents. Almost five thousand people died and publisher Mathew Carey, who lived in Philadelphia at the time, estimated that

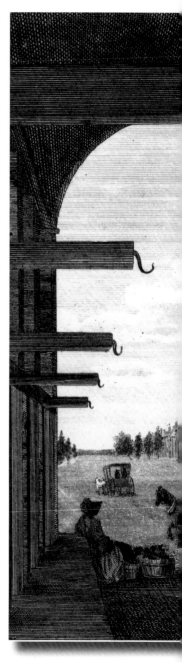

This view from the late 1790s shows High Street from the Country Market in Philadelphia. Philadelphia, the capital of the United States in 1793, turned into a virtual ghost town during the yellow fever epidemic, when most of its residents fled from the outbreak.

another seventeen thousand people had fled the city.

Woven throughout the historically accurate tale of the fever itself, Anderson tells the story of fourteen-year-old Mattie Cook. Mattie, her mother, and her war-hero grandfather run the Cook Coffeehouse. When their serving girl and Mattie's childhood friend, Polly, dies of the fever, Mattie's mother sends her out of the city in an effort to prevent her from becoming infected. Soon, however, Mattie is forced to return to the ravaged city. But there is no sign of her mother. As the months pass with Mattie unsure whether or not her mother has survived the epidemic, she is forced to make adult decisions to keep herself and the family business alive.

Anderson told Reading Rockets that she got the idea for the book from a newspaper article

In 2004, *Fever 1793* was adapted into a stage play by Steve Braddock, who is shown here with Anderson at LeMoyne College's Coyne Center for the Performing Arts in Syracuse, New York.

that was commemorating the two-hundredth anniversary of the outbreak. "I'm a big history geek. And I had never heard about this epidemic," she said. The article sparked her imagination and she started research at the Pennsylvania Historical Society. She told Reading Rockets that she found out many years later that Jim Murphy, author of the nonfiction book *An American Plague: The True and Terrifying Story of the Yellow Fever Epidemic of 1793*, which is often taught alongside Anderson's *Fever 1793* in classrooms, was doing research at the Pennsylvania Historical Society at the same time she was. "[H]e must have seen the same article," she says.

All together, seven years passed between the time Anderson saw that newspaper article in 1993 and *Fever 1793*'s publication date in 2000. So much time had passed because *Fever 1793* required a lot of research, and Anderson wrote *Speak* after finishing the first draft of the historical novel. Several years after the book was published, it was adapted into a stage play. In May 2004, it was performed at the Gifford Family Theater in Syracuse, New York.

Anderson's readers seem to respond on a visceral level to her historical novels. She told *School Library Journal* that one of her favorite fan letters she has gotten was from a sixth-grade girl in

New Jersey whose "father had been in the Twin Towers on 9/11. He had survived, but she identified with [Mattie's] feelings of panic and disaster and being out of control and the world suddenly not being safe."

SEEDS OF AMERICA TRILOGY

While writing *Fever 1793*, Anderson came across the fact that Benjamin Franklin, one of her heroes, had been a slave owner. "I was shocked!" she told Reading Rockets. "No one ever taught me that!" In all the books she had read about Franklin, Anderson says she remembers them being called "servants" instead of slaves.

When she investigated further, Anderson found that Franklin had indeed owned as many as seven people from 1735 to 1781. She also found that he ran ads to expose runaway slaves and helped return them to their owners. She continued to dig and found more and more references to slave owners in the North. She told Reading Rockets that this confused her. She had been taught that it was mainly Southerners who owned slaves. But through her research, she found that slavery was "insidious and widespread" in the North as well.

This fact eventually led to Anderson writing *Chains* several years later. Published in 2008, *Chains* is the first in the Revolutionary War trilogy

titled *Seeds of America.* The story is about thirteen-year-old Isabel and her sister, Ruth. Isabel and Ruth are slaves promised freedom by their kindly owner upon her death. However, a dishonest relative defies his aunt's wishes and denies the girls their freedom, instead selling them to a Loyalist couple from New York City. There, Isabel meets Curzon, a slave with Patriot ties. Isabel struggles to protect her younger sister and keep them together while trying to determine which side

Anderson was horrified to find out that Benjamin Franklin had owned slaves in the mid-1700s. He later had a change of heart and joined an abolitionist group, which sought to end slavery.

is most likely to give her freedom. Sadly, while the fight for American freedom raged, both sides largely ignored the freedom of the slaves.

Forge, published in 2010, is the second book in the *Seeds of America* trilogy and focuses on fifteen-year-old Curzon as he fights against the British at Valley Forge. According to an update to Anderson's Facebook page on January 17, 2013, she is in the middle of researching *Ashes*, the final installment of the trilogy. As of June 2013, no publication date had been set for *Ashes*.

BOOKS FOR YOUNG READERS

Although better known for her young adult fiction and historical thrillers, Anderson has also written books for the younger crowd. She began writing picture books when her children were little, and her first published book was a picture book titled *Ndito Runs*.

PICTURE BOOKS

Ndito Runs is about a young Kenyan girl who runs miles to get to and from school every day. As she runs, Ndito imagines that she is different animals—a soaring crane, a galloping wildebeest, or a hopping dik-dik, to name a few. In a biography of Anderson on the Scholastic Web site, she says she got the idea for *Ndito Runs* from a National Public Radio (NPR) story about Kenyan Olympic marathon runners. *Ndito Runs* was

published in 1996 and has been translated into four South African languages: Xhosa, Zulu, Africaans, and Sotho.

Other than *Ndito Runs*, which Anderson characterizes as a "quiet, gentle" book, she told Reading Rockets that her other picture books fall into one of two categories—they are either "rowdy, exaggerated stories for little kids" or ones that include "historical events depicted in a way that makes them interesting."

Her second picture book, *Turkey Pox*, was released in the fall of 1996, several months after *Ndito Runs* was published. Her Scholastic biography reveals that the inspiration for *Turkey Pox* was her daughter Meredith's bout with chickenpox. When the four-year-old broke out in spots on Thanksgiving Day, Anderson changed her Thanksgiving plans. But she also thought, "Man, this is going to be a great story!," Patricia Newman reported in *California Kids!*

Two years later, in 1998, the characters introduced in *Turkey Pox* make another appearance in *No Time for Mother's Day*. This time, Charity, the little girl, is searching for something to give her mom on Mother's Day. After watching her mother's frantic schedule one Saturday, Charity comes up with the perfect gift when she decides to turn off "everything that beeps or bleeps or buzzes."

GENRE JUMPING

Anderson is often asked why she jumps around to so many different genres within the children's market. She told Reading Rockets that the reason is very simple: "I have a very short attention span." In actuality, like many people, Anderson has a short attention span for some things—television, for example—but she can concentrate on things that interest her for much longer periods of time. She told Reading Rockets that when she finds something that really fascinates her, she can spend hours and hours on it.

She told Susie Wilde of *AudioFile* magazine, "I love jumping back and forth between the forms. I think it keeps each book fresh and exciting for me because I don't have to grind out the same old, same old all the time." Her method seems to be working.

Anderson's fourth picture book, *The Big Cheese of Third Street*, was published in 2002. The story is about pint-sized Benny Antonelli, who is so small that he gets thrown around like a ball, swept up with the trash, and dumped in a salad when his aunt mistakes him for a tomato. In the end, Benny gets his just rewards when he scampers to the top of the greased pole at the annual block party and grabs the prize: the cheese at the top. In her Scholastic biography, Anderson calls this book her "salute to [my] adopted hometown of Philadelphia."

Following the publication of *Fever 1793*, one of Anderson's editors at Simon & Schuster, knowing how much she loves Thanksgiving, suggested that she investigate the life of Sarah Josepha Hale. This idea led to the research and writing of her first nonfiction picture book, *Thank You Sarah: The Woman Who Saved Thanksgiving*, which was published in 2002. Sarah Josepha Hale was an American author who launched and pursued (for years!) a letter-writing campaign that eventually made Thanksgiving an American holiday.

by L

THANK YOU, *Sarah!*

The Woman
Who Saved
Thanksgiving

Hmmph.

...lse Anderson   illustrated by **Matt Faulkner**

Sarah Josepha Hale *(far left)*, the subject of Anderson's first nonfiction picture book *(above)*, was an American writer and editor whose influence and persistence helped make Thanksgiving a national holiday.

Anderson also reveals on her blog that, while researching her family genealogy, she found that Hale was a distant relative. Incidentally, Sarah Josepha Hale is also the author of the nursery rhyme *Mary Had a Little Lamb*.

On her blog, Anderson relates the tale that her editors at Simon & Schuster were so happy with the way *Thank You Sarah* turned out that they asked if she had any other ideas for a similar book. As a matter of fact, she did! In the mid-1990s, pre-published Anderson researched and wrote a proposal for a book that would highlight six women and girls who were instrumental in the Revolutionary War. Everyone she sent the proposal to rejected it, but Anderson did not throw her research away.

Now was her chance to put that research to use. She pitched the book to her editors. They liked the idea, but they wanted her to include more than six women and girls. Anderson went home and researched some more, eventually coming up with eighty-nine profiles of women involved in the American Revolution. The result was *Independent Dames: What You Never Knew About the Women and Girls of the American Revolution*. So much research went into the book, it "was almost like writing a novel," she told Reading Rockets.

Anderson's picture book *The Hair of Zoe Fleefenbacher Goes to School* was published in

bigail Adams is just one of the eighty-nine independent dames depicted in
nderson's picture book about the women and girls who played a part in the
merican Revolution.

2009 and promptly became a *New York Times* best seller. Zoe's red hair is so big that it fills the entire room. It has a mind of its own, too. Zoe's parents think that her hair is beautiful. Her kindergarten teacher finds it charming. But Ms. Trisk, her first-grade teacher, is having none of it. "School has rules," she says. "No wild hair in my class!" Zoe's hair is a metaphor for her "wild, lovely, energetic child nature," Anderson told Reading Rockets. She dedicated the book to her daughter Meredith, who became a middle school science teacher the year it was published.

VET VOLUNTEERS

"I started writing as a young mom. And as my children got older, my interests and tastes got older, too," Anderson told Reading Rockets. In 2000, American Girl published the first volume in a new elementary chapter book series, called *Wild at Heart*, written by Anderson. Anderson describes the series as "a mix of *Babysitter's Club* and *Animal ER*." The stories are about a group of eleven-year-olds who volunteer at the Wild at Heart Veterinary Clinic, a dream job for her ten-year-old self, Anderson told Reading Rockets.

Like her books for teens, the *Wild at Heart* series does not shy away from tough issues. The books touch on topics such as illegal puppy mills, the imminent death of a beloved pet, and adjusting to the need for a service dog. Anderson told Reading Rockets that she writes about such harsh realities for middle grade students for the same reason she writes about them for teens: "Real things happen to ten-year-olds," she says.

Anderson also told Reading Rockets that some of her favorite fan mail comes from the readers of these books. She really loves animals, but she has terrible allergies. Many of her fans send her pictures of their pets, which allow her to get close to the animals without getting sick.

Puffin rereleased the series under the name *Vet Volunteers* in the late 2000s, and in October 2009, Anderson announced on her blog that the first two books had been translated into Japanese.

SIX

LIVING AND LOVING THE LITERARY LIFE

As if she is not busy enough with her young adult novels, historical thrillers, picture books, and chapter books, Anderson also stays busy by contributing short stories and essays to different anthologies from time to time. Her first short story, "Passport," was published the year before *Speak* came out.

ESSAYS, SHORT STORIES, AND OTHER WRITING

"Passport" was Anderson's contribution to *Dirty Laundry: Stories About Family Secrets.* This short story tells the tale of eighteen-year-old Jared, who is desperately trying to negotiate the "Land of Mom" and the "Kingdom of Dad" after his parents divorce and the battle lines are drawn. His mother is pushing college applications on him while his father is determined that Jared will go into the army. Jared, however, has other plans altogether. Short stories by Richard Peck (*A Year Down Yonder*), M. E. Kerr (*Dinky Hocker Shoots Smack!*), and Rita Williams-Garcia (*One Crazy Summer*) also appear in the collection.

Another of Anderson's short stories, "Snake," can be found in *Love & Sex: Ten Stories of Truth.* This story is about two young adults, both on the cusp of leading their own lives, who are roped into a forced blind date by their fathers, who are business associates. Lily's father is dragging her around the country in his grand tour of all his carpet stores. In every city, her father sets her up with one of his employee's sons and she is sick of it. When they get to California, it is Adam's turn. Adam's father is angling for a promotion to regional director of the area's carpet stores. Both Lily and Adam are uncomfortable and resentful as their respective fathers dress them up like dolls and send them on their way. Only when Lily and Adam get past their expectations can they really see each other and find, to their surprise, that they actually have a lot in common. Joan Bauer (*Hope Was Here*), Garth Nix (*Sabriel*), and Sonya Sones (*What My Mother Doesn't Know*) are a few of the other contributors to this collection.

Mexico, a town in upstate New York, where Anderson lives, gets a lot of snow in winter. In her essay in *Recycle This Book*, Anderson shares some tips on how she and her family save energy even when the snow piles up outside their home.

Dear Author: Letters of Hope is a collection of letters to young adult authors and their responses to their readers. This book includes a letter from a reader who experienced a similar type of sexual assault as Melinda in *Speak*. Anderson responds to the correspondent's bravery in finding her voice and coming out of the darkness. Other young adult authors, including Chris Crutcher (*Staying Fat for Sarah Byrnes*), Jerry Spinelli (*Stargirl*), and Christopher Paul Curtis (*The Watsons Go to Birmingham—1963*), also share messages from their readers.

In *Recycle This Book: 100 Top Children's Book Authors Tell You How to Go Green*, Anderson's essay reveals the ways in which she tries to be mindful about her use of nonrenewable energy sources. She explains, for example, that she and her husband made the conscious decision to drive cars that get very good gas mileage. They also save gasoline by planning out their week and attempting to lump all their errands into one trip. Though they live in an area that gets copious amounts of snow, the couple saves fuel by setting their heat to 60 degrees Fahrenheit (15.6 degrees Celsius). They keep the house warm with a wood-burning fireplace designed to give off maximum heat. Because they live in upstate New York, the summer heat is not as much of a problem as the winter cold, so they do not own an air conditioner. If it gets too hot in the summer,

THE WRITING COTTAGE

In keeping with her environmental awareness, Anderson's writing cottage—built by her husband Scot Larrabee, a carpenter, and their friends—is made completely of recycled and sustainable materials. Shortly after construction began on the cottage in 2009, one of their friends told Anderson and Larrabee about an old window leaning against a

barn about an hour and a half from their home. The window, which was salvaged from a church built in the late 1800s, sported a large, round piece of glass in the center and eight smaller round windows surrounding it. In her YouTube video detailing the construction of the cottage, Anderson calls it her "magic window" and it quickly became a focal point for the cottage's construction.

The cottage is warmed by the use of a wood stove and the proper application of soybean-based foam insulation. In fact, the cottage is completely off-grid, which means that it is self-sufficient and does not draw electricity from the power company. Instead, a windmill and solar panels on the roof provide the electricity that Anderson needs while she writes.

She relies on the cottage to sustain her, too. "While I love traveling and meeting readers and fellow writers, the truth is that I am deeply introverted. Spending time around other people drains all the creativity and ink from my soul. The solitude of my cottage in the woods helps refill it," she told Jolie Stekley on Stekley's blog, *Cuppa Jolie*.

Anderson sits with her laptop, in front of her "magic window," while working on *Forge*. Her husband and some of his friends built the writing cottage for Anderson.

Anderson says, they simply retreat to the basement of the house, where it is cooler. She also makes a point of buying only locally grown and raised food products, and she freezes and cans fruits and vegetables when they are in season. These actions prevent food from having to be shipped from far away, using fossil fuels in the process. Why go to all the trouble? "We want the seventh generation of the seventh generation of our children to live in health and abundance in a world that has been restored to balance," Anderson says.

WINNING AWARDS

Over the years, Anderson's commitment to the literature of young people has been recognized with many awards and honors. *Speak* and *Chains* were both National Book Award finalists in 1999 and 2008, respectively. This prestigious literary award is given to writers by writers, which means that a panel of young adult authors judges the young adult books that are nominated. *When Zachary Beaver Came to Town* by Kimberly Willis Holt won the young people's literature award in 1999, and Judy Blundell's *What I Saw and How I Lied* was the winner in 2008.

Along with being a National Book Award finalist in 1999, *Speak* was also honored with the Society of Children's Books Writers and Illustrators (SCBWI)

Chains was a National Book Award Nominee for Young People's Literature in 2008 and the winner of the Scott O'Dell Award for Historical Fiction in 2009.

Golden Kite Award for Fiction. In 2000, the book was an Edgar Award Nominee for Best Young Adult, a Printz Honor book, and listed as an ALA Top Ten Best Books for Young Adults.

Speak certainly is not the only one of Anderson's books that has won awards either. In 2009, *Chains* received the Scott O'Dell Award for Historical Fiction. Children's writer Scott O'Dell (*The Island of the Blue Dolphins*) established this award to encourage other children's writers to focus on writing exciting, engaging historical fiction for young people. *Chains* was also named as an ALA Notable Children's Book for Older Readers that year.

Along with the individual awards for specific books, Anderson has also been the recipient of some of the most prestigious awards in the young adult literary world. In 2008, she was awarded the Assembly on Literature for Adolescents (ALAN) Award for outstanding contributions in the field of adolescent literature. She is in good company: renowned young adult authors such as S. E. Hinton (*The Outsiders*), Gary Paulsen (*Hatchet*), and Madeleine L'Engle (*A Wrinkle in Time*) have been ALAN award recipients.

A year later, the American Library Association honored Anderson with the Margaret A. Edwards Award. This award is supervised by the Young Adult Library Services Association and sponsored by

School Library Journal. Like the ALAN award, the Edwards Award honors an author's body of work for "significant and lasting contribution to young adult literature." She was granted the Edwards Award based on *Catalyst*, *Fever 1793*, and *Speak*. The awards committee said of Anderson's work, "These gripping and exceptionally well-written novels, through various settings, time periods, and circumstances, poignantly reflect the growing and changing realities facing teens. Iconic and classic in her storytelling and character development, Anderson has created for teens a body of work that continues to be widely read and cherished by a diverse audience."

THE BEST JOB ON EARTH

From her very first book, Anderson's commitment to speaking up for young people, as well as teaching them to speak for themselves, shines through in her work. She told *Teacher Librarian* that she writes about the harsh realities of teenage life "because I care about teenagers." She went on to say that she remembers her adolescent years and how overwhelming they can be. She said she sometimes wishes that she could write books that are lighter in tone, more "happy" books, but "then I get amazing letters from readers who tell me that one of my books helped them get through a tough

Sherman Alexie, author of *The Absolutely True Diary of a Part-Time Indian*, is one of the contemporary young adult authors whom Anderson enjoys reading when she gets a chance.

time, and I know that this is what I am meant to do."

Like many writers, Anderson is a prodigious reader. However, she does not normally read contemporary young adult novels while she is working on one, she told Reading Rockets. She is worried that if she reads a book with a really compelling character in it, that character might inadvertently slip into one of her books. Nonetheless, if she is working on other projects, she might pick up a current young adult novel. One of her favorites, she told Reading Rockets, is Sherman Alexie's *The Absoutely True Diary of a Part-Time Indian.* She also mentioned *Holes*, *Weetzie Bat*, *The Golden Compass*, and *The Watsons Go to Birmingham, 1963* as some of her favorite children's books. She enjoys reading mysteries written for adults and mentions P. D. James as a favorite author, too. Reading nonfiction, including biographies, for research purposes and for pleasure is another favorite pastime.

Anderson told Debbi Michiko Florence that her favorite parts of being a writer are "living in my imagination, working in [my] pajamas, [and] proximity to refrigerator." The downside she says is "boring grown-up junk. Mostly, it's a blast."

Hopefully, that means that Anderson will continue to deliver her heartfelt, realistic teen fiction, as well as historically accurate historical thrillers, for many years to come. She told *Teacher Librarian*, "Storytelling is the age-old, traditional vehicle for passing along wisdom. I hope my books make readers smile and maybe help them take a few more steps toward adulthood without stumbling."

ON LAURIE HALSE ANDERSON

Birth date: October 23, 1961

Birthplace: Potsdam, New York

Current residence: Mexico, New York

First publication: *Ndito Runs* (New York, NY: Henry Holt & Company, 1996)

Marital status: Greg Anderson, 1983–2002; Scot Larrabee, 2004–present

Children: 4, Stephanie Holcomb (1985) and Meredith Lauren (1987), stepmom to Jessica and Christian Larrabee

High schools attended: Fayetteville-Manlius High School, Manlius, New York; Høng HF og Studenterkursus, Denmark

Colleges attended: Onondaga County Community College, Syracuse, New York; Georgetown University, Washington, D.C.

Motto: "It's not a mistake if you learn from it."

Favorite authors: P. D. James, Neil Gaiman, Elizabeth George

Five favorite books: *American Gods* by Neil Gaiman, *Weetzie Bat* by Francesca Lia Block, *The Time*

Traveler's Wife by Audrey Niffenegger, *The Artist's Way* by Julia Cameron, and *Common Sense* by Thomas Paine

Interests: Running and American history

Previous occupations: Anderson has been a newspaper reporter and journalist, and she has worked on a dairy farm and a pig farm.

Awards and honors: 2008 ALAN Award for outstanding contributions in the field of adolescent literature; 2009 Margaret A. Edwards Award

ON LAURIE HALSE ANDERSON'S WORK

YOUNG ADULT

Speak. New York, NY: Farrar, Straus and Giroux, 1999.

Synopsis: High school freshman Melinda Sordino finds herself cast out of her group of friends and roundly hated by upperclassmen she doesn't even know after she calls the police to an end-of-summer party. What they don't know, and what Melinda cannot tell them, is that something horrible happened at that party. Something Melinda cannot voice.

Awards: National Book Award Nominee for Young People's Literature (1999), Golden Kite Award for Fiction (1999), BCCB Blue Ribbon Book (1999), Edgar Award Nominee for Best Young Adult (2000), Michael L. Printz Honor (2000), South Carolina Book Award for Young Adult Book Award (2002), Horn Book Fanfare (2000), ALA's Top Ten Best Books for Young Adults (2000), Abraham Lincoln Award Nominee (2005)

Catalyst. New York, NY: Viking Juvenile, 2002.

Synopsis: Kate Malone is a smart, driven high school senior waiting for her acceptance letter to MIT. She has it all under control, or so she thinks, until her next-door neighbor and childhood nemesis, Teri Litch, moves in and takes over her bedroom. After that, the events in her life unfold like an out-of-control, explosive chemical reaction.

Award: ALA's Top Ten Best Books for Young Adults (2003)

Prom New York, NY: Viking Juvenile, 2005.

Synopsis: High school senior and cynic Ashley Hannigan could care less about going to the prom. All she wants to do is finish school and start her real life. But when her best friend, Natalia, begs for her help after a teacher steals the prom fund, Ashley finds that she cannot say no and winds up in the middle of all the preparations.

Twisted. New York, NY: Viking Juvenile, 2007.

Synopsis: Tyler Miller is tired of fading into the woodwork, so he decides to do something to get himself noticed. He succeeds—especially with the police. After a summer of hard labor to fulfill his probation, he begins his senior year sporting a new bad-boy reputation. When he also attracts the attention of the most popular girl in school (and his secret crush), he thinks maybe all the trouble was worthwhile—at least until things begin to go bad and his bad-boy reputation becomes more than he can handle.

Awards: South Carolina Book Award Nominee for Young Adult Book Award (2010), ALA Teens' Top Ten (2008), Michigan Library Association Thumbs Up! Award Nominee (2008), Abraham Lincoln Award Nominee (2011)

Wintergirls. New York, NY: Viking Juvenile, 2009.

Synopsis: Lia and Cassie are best friends and they have a bet. They bet that they can be the skinniest girls in school. But when their contest ends with one of them dead, the other must learn how to live or risk following her friend to the grave.

Awards: Romantic Times (RT) Reviewers' Choice Award Nominee for Best Young Adult Novel (2009), An ALA/YALSA Quick Pick for Reluctant Young Adult Readers (2010), Cybils Award Nominee for Young Adult Fiction (2009), TAYSHAS High School Reading List (2010), Goodreads Choice Award Nominee for Young Adult Fiction (2009), ALA Teens' Top Ten (2010), Milwaukee County Teen Book Award (2010), Michigan Library Association Thumbs Up! Award Nominee (2010), Iowa High School Book Award Nominee (2011)

HISTORICAL FICTION

Fever 1793. New York, NY: Simon & Schuster Books for Young Readers, 2000.

Synopsis: In the summer of 1793, fourteen-year-old Mattie Cook is more concerned with how to grow her family's small coffeehouse into a thriving business than she is of the growing rumors of a fever. However, when her mother contracts the disease, Mattie's attention must shift to the struggle to survive the epidemic outbreak and its aftermath.

Award: Rebecca Caudill Young Reader's Book Award (2003)

Chains (*Seeds of America* #1). New York, NY: Atheneum Books for Young Readers, 2008.

Synopsis: Thirteen-year-old Isabel and her little sister, Ruth, were supposed to be freed. But when their benevolent owner dies, an unscrupulous relative sells the two girls to a Loyalist couple with no sympathy for the Patriots of the American Revolution. When something horrible happens to Ruth, Isabel decides that her loyalty will lie with whichever side offers her freedom. But exactly which side is that?

Awards: National Book Award Nominee for Young People's Literature (2008), Scott O'Dell Award (2009), Cybils Award for Middle Grade Fiction

(2009), An ALA Notable Children's Book for Older Readers (2009), Rebecca Caudill Young Reader's Book Award Nominee (2011), South Carolina Book Award Nominee for Junior Book Award (2011), TAYSHAS High School Reading List (2010)

Forge (*Seeds of America* #2). New York, NY: Atheneum Books for Young Readers, 2010.

Synopsis: In this sequel to *Chains*, Curzon joins the Patriot Army under false pretenses—an escaped slave passing as free. If he is caught, he knows that either side can sell him to the slave traders. Who can he trust? He should he not? And will he ever be truly free?

Awards: YALSA Best Fiction for Young Adults (2011), NAIBA Book of the Year for Middle Readers (2011)

Ashes (*Seeds of America* #3). Publication to be determined

NONFICTION FOR YOUNG READERS

Thank You, Sarah!: The Woman Who Saved Thanksgiving. New York, NY: Simon & Schuster Books for Young Readers, 2002.

Synopsis: *Thank You, Sarah!* is the story of Sarah Josepha Hale, an American writer and editor who, with her persistent letter writing campaign, persuaded President Abraham Lincoln to declare Thanksgiving a national holiday in 1863.

Award: Once Upon a World Children's Book Award (2003)

Independent Dames: What You Never Knew About the Women and Girls of the American Revolution. New York, NY: Simon & Schuster Books for Young Readers, 2008.

Synopsis: *Independent Dames* shines the light on eighty-nine women and girls of the American Revolution who are often left in the dark in traditional history books.

FICTION FOR YOUNG READERS

Vet Volunteer Series:

Fight for Life (Vet Volunteers #1). New York, NY: Puffin Books, 2007.

Homeless (Vet Volunteers #2). New York, NY: Puffin Books, 2007.

Trickster (Vet Volunteers #3). New York, NY: Puffin Books, 2008.

Manatee Blues (Vet Volunteers #4). New York, NY: Puffin Books, 2008.

Say Good-Bye (Vet Volunteers #5). New York, NY: Puffin Books, 2008.

Storm Rescue (Vet Volunteers #6). New York, NY: Puffin
    Books, 2008.
Teacher's Pet (Vet Volunteers #7). New York, NY: Puffin
    Books, 2009.
Trapped (Vet Volunteers #8). New York, NY: Puffin
    Books, 2009.
Fear of Falling (Vet Volunteers #9). New York, NY: Puffin
    Books, 2009.
Time to Fly (Vet Volunteers #10). New York, NY: Puffin
    Books, 2009.
Masks (Vet Volunteers #11). New York, NY: Puffin
    Books, 2012.
End of the Race (Vet Volunteers #12). New York, NY:
    Puffin Books, 2012.
New Beginnings (Vet Volunteers #13). New York, NY:
    Puffin Books, 2012.
Acting Out (Vet Volunteers #14). New York, NY: Puffin
    Books, 2012.
Helping Hands (Vet Volunteers #15). New York, NY:
    Puffin Books, 2013.

PICTURE BOOKS

Ndito Runs. New York, NY: Henry Holt & Company, 1996.
Turkey Pox. Chicago, IL: Albert Whitman &
    Company, 1996.
No Time for Mother's Day. Chicago, IL: Albert Whitman
    & Company, 1998.

The Big Cheese of Third Street. New York, NY: Simon & Schuster Children's Publishing, 2002.

The Hair of Zoe Fleefenbacher Goes to School. New York, NY: Simon & Schuster Books for Young Readers, 2009.

ANTHOLOGY CONTRIBUTIONS

Fraustino, Lisa Rowe (ed.). *Dirty Laundry: Stories About Family Secrets.* New York, NY: Viking Books, 1998.

Cart, Michael (ed.). *Love & Sex: Ten Stories of Truth.* New York, NY: Simon & Schuster Children's Publishing, 2001.

Kaywell, Joan (ed.). *Dear Author: Letters of Hope* (*Top Young Adult Authors Respond to Kids' Toughest Issues*). New York, NY: Philomel Books, 2007.

Gutman, Dan (ed.). *Recycle This Book: 100 Top Children's Book Authors Tell You How to Go Green.* New York, NY: Yearling Books, 2009.

Speak (1999)

"In her YA fiction debut, Anderson perfectly captures the harsh conformity of high school cliques and one teen's struggle to find acceptance from her peers. Melinda's sarcastic wit, honesty, and courage make her a memorable character whose ultimate triumph will inspire and empower readers."—Debbie Carton, *Booklist*, September 15, 1999

Fever 1793 (2000)

"Extremely well researched, Anderson's novel paints a vivid picture of the seedy waterfront, the devastation the disease wreaks on a once thriving city, and the bitterness of neighbor toward neighbor as those suspected of infection are physically cast aside. However, these larger scale views take precedence over the kind of intimate scenes that Anderson crafted so masterfully in *Speak*."—*Publishers Weekly*, July 31, 2000

Catalyst (2002)

"An unlikely friendship as a catalyst for change is a common element of adolescent literature, but Anderson's take on human relations succeeds through her fresh writing and exceptional characterization."—Lauren Adams, *The Horn Book Magazine*, November–December 2002

CRITICAL REVIEWS

Prom (2005)

"Anderson, the award-winning author of *Speak* and other serious YA novels, has concocted a delightful confection here, full of laughs, warmth, and teenage dialog so true to life you might have heard it in the hall on the way to math class."—Paula Rohrlick, *Kliatt*, March 2005

Twisted (2007)

"Anderson returns to weightier issues in the style of her most revered work, *Speak* (1999), and stretches her wings by offering up a male protagonist for the first time. As tension mounts, Tyler reaches a crisis point revealed through one of the most poignant and gripping scenes in young-adult literature. Taking matters into his own hands, Tyler decides that he must make a choice about what kind of man he wants to be, with or without his father's guidance."—*Kirkus Reviews*, February 15, 2007

Independent Dames: What You Never Knew About the Women and Girls of the American Revolution (2007)

"A jam-packed, busy presentation overwhelms this otherwise fresh exploration of women's contributions to the War of Independence. Anderson sure has done her homework, digging out names and particulars of a dizzying number of strong women from the expected—Phillis Wheatley, Abigail Adams—to the lesser known—Sally St. Clair, Tyonajanegen—working to ensure occupational and ethnic diversity throughout."—*Kirkus Reviews*, May 15, 2008

Chains (2008)

"Anderson (*Speak*; *Fever 1793*) packs so much detail into her evocation of wartime New York City that readers will see the turmoil and confusion of the times, and her solidly researched exploration of British and Patriot treatment of slaves during a war for freedom is nuanced and evenhanded, presented in service of a fast-moving, emotionally involving plot."—*Publishers Weekly*, September 1, 2008

The Hair of Zoe Fleefenbacher Goes to School (2009)

"Anderson's narrative sparkles with exuberant language and exaggerated humor. Hoyt's buoyant cartoons, done in pen and ink and watercolors, are filled with flowing lines and comical touches. An imaginative and appealing back-to-school choice."—Joy Fleishhacker, *School Library Journal*, August 2009

Wintergirls (2009)

"Anderson conveys Lia's illness vividly through her dark, fantastic thoughts—full of images of tangled, spiky vegetation and continuous, bitter rejection of her parents. To read this stream-of-consciousness, first-person, present-tense work is to be drawn into an anorexic mentality (grotesque descriptions of food, calories assigned to every morsel), and therefore not for every reader, though it makes for a tense, illuminating tale."—Deirdre F. Baker, *The Horn Book Magazine*, March–April 2009

Forge (2010)

"When it comes to background research, Anderson has clearly and commendably done her work. It is difficult to imagine there will ever be historical fiction about this time in America that is more nuanced or respectful of time and place."—Jerry Griswold, *The New York Times Book Review*, February 13, 2011

1961 Laurie Beth Halse is born in Potsdam, New York.

1983 Laurie Halse marries Greg Anderson.

1985 Oldest daughter, Stephanie Holcomb, is born.

1987 Second child, Meredith Lauren, is born.

1996 Anderson's first book, a picture book, titled *Ndito Runs*, is published, closely followed by a second picture book, *Turkey Pox*.

1998 *No Time for Mother's Day* is published.

1999 Anderson's first young adult novel, *Speak*, is published.

2000 The first book in the *Vet Volunteer* series is published.

2002 Anderson's first historical thriller, *Fever 1793*, and her first nonfiction picture book, *Thank You, Sarah!: The Woman Who Saved Thanksgiving*, are published. Her second young adult novel, *Catalyst*, and her fourth picture book, *The Big Cheese of Third Street*, are also published. Laurie and Greg Anderson divorce.

2004 Anderson marries childhood friend Scot Larrabee and is inducted into the Fayetteville-Manlius Hall of Distinction.

2006 Anderson awarded Onondaga Community College Alumni Faces Award.

2008 Anderson awarded ALAN Award for outstanding contributions in the field of adolescent literature. Her second nonfiction picture book, *Independent*

Dames: What You Never Knew About the Women and Girls of the American Revolution, and her second historical thriller, *Chains*, are published.

2009 Anderson receives the Margaret A. Edwards Award. The picture book *The Hair of Zoe Fleefenbacher Goes to School* and young adult novel *Wintergirls* are published.

2010 The second book in the *Seeds of America* series, *Forge*, is published. Anderson is chosen as School Library Month Spokesperson for the American Association of School Librarians (AASL), a division of the American Library Association (ALA).

2012 The thirteenth and fourteenth books of the *Vet Volunteers* series are published.

2013 Anderson completes another young adult novel and is researching the final book in the *Seeds of America* trilogy, *Ashes*.

ANTHOLOGY A collection of short stories, essays, poems, or other literary pieces.

ASSOCIATE'S DEGREE A two-year college degree.

CAMEO A brief appearance.

CATALYST A substance that increases the rate of a chemical reaction.

CENSORSHIP The attempt to remove or suppress material one finds objectionable or offensive.

COMMEMORATE To honor the memory of.

CONTROVERSY A public argument.

ENDURING Lasting.

GENEALOGY The investigation of family history and relationships.

GENRE A distinct form of literature (or music or art) marked by a particular style or content.

HAIKU An unrhymed poem consisting of three lines containing five, seven, and five syllables.

ICONIC Important and enduring.

INDEPENDENT FILM A film that is produced mostly outside of a major motion-picture studio.

INNATE Inborn or natural.

INSIDIOUS Proceeding in a subtle and gradual manner with harmful effects.

LINGUISTICS The study of the nature and structure of language.

LITERARY DEVICE A technique or method used for effect in a piece of writing.

LOYALIST An American colonist who remained loyal to the British crown during the American Revolution.

MARGINALIZE To treat someone or something as insignificant or unimportant.

MORALITY Ideas or principles concerning the distinction between right and wrong.

NEMESIS A formidable opponent or enemy.

PARIAH A social outcast.

PATRIOT An American colonist who rebelled against the British during the American Revolution.

PERSISTENCE The act of not giving up on something.

PERSPECTIVE A point of view or outlook.

PLAUSIBLE Believable.

POIGNANT Profoundly moving.

PREMIERE The first public performance or showing of something, such as a musical, stage play, or film.

PRESTIGIOUS Impressive or influential.

PRIMARY SOURCE A direct source of information created during the period under study.

PROTAGONIST The main character.

REVISION The act of editing or rewriting a literary work.

SAGA A novel about several generations or members of a family.

SPEECH IMPEDIMENT A disorder that disrupts normal speech.

SUSTAINABLE Capable of being used over time with minimal harm to the environment.

SYMBOLISM The use of a person, place, object, or action to represent an abstract idea.

TOLERANCE The recognition and respect of other people's opinions or beliefs.

UNRELIABLE NARRATOR A narrator who cannot be trusted to be completely truthful.

VET To verify or check for accuracy.

VISCERAL Relating to deep or instinctual feelings about something.

VORACIOUS Having a very eager or greedy approach to something.

AFS-USA (formerly American Field Service)
One Whitehall Street, 2nd Floor
New York, NY 10004
(800) 237-4636
Web site: http://www.afsusa.org
The AFS-USA organizes international high school
    student-exchange programs.

Anti-Censorship Center
1111 West Kenyon Road
Urbana, IL 61801-1096
(217) 328-3870
Web site: http://www.ncte.org/action/anti-censorship
The Anti-Censorship Center is part of the National
    Council of Teachers of English (NCTE). Its Web
    site provides model procedures for responding
    to challenges, criteria and procedures for select-
    ing materials for English class, and rationales for
    teaching challenged books.

Canadian Association of Sexual Assault Centres
    (CASAC)
77 East 20th Avenue
Vancouver, BC V5V 1L7
Canada
(604) 876-2622
Web site: http://www.casac.ca
The CASAC is a group of rape crisis centers and
    women's shelters throughout Canada whose goal
    is to carry out the legal, social, and attitudinal

changes necessary to prevent, and ultimately eradicate, rape and sexual assault.

Laurie Halse Anderson
P.O. Box 906
Mexico, NY 13114
Web site: http://madwomanintheforest.com
This address can be used to contact Laurie Halse Anderson directly.

National Book Foundation
90 Broad Street, Suite 604
New York, NY 10004
(212) 685-0261
Web site: http://www.nationalbook.org
The National Book Foundation presents the prestigious National Book Awards, including the one for young people's literature. All the National Book Award winners and nominees can be found on its Web site.

National Coalition Against Censorship (NCAC)
19 Fulton Street, Suite 407
New York, NY 10038
(212) 807-6222
Web site: http://www.ncac.org
The NCAC is dedicated to providing educational resources and advocacy support for people facing censorship or other actions that threaten free expression. It has many ongoing projects,

including the Kid's Right to Read Project, which provides advice and assistance to students, teachers, and others opposing book banning in schools and communities.

National Eating Disorders Association (NEDA)
165 West 46th Street
New York, NY 10036
(212) 575-6200
Web site: https://www.nationaleatingdisorders.org
The NEDA provides support and education for individuals struggling with an eating disorder and their families. Its Web site provides toolkits for parents and educators who want to know more about the signs, symptoms, and medical consequences of eating disorders.

National Eating Disorder Information Centre (NEDIC)
S 7-421, 200 Elizabeth Street
Toronto, ON M5G 2C4
Canada
(416) 340-4156
Web site: http://www.nedic.ca/drupal/node/2
The NEDIC is a nonprofit Canadian organization that provides educational resources about eating disorders and staffs a telephone helpline [(866) 633-4220] that provides information on treatment and support.

Rape, Abuse, and Incest National Network (RAINN)
2000 L Street NW, Suite 406

Washington, DC 20036
(202) 544-3064
Web site: http://www.rainn.org
RAINN is America's largest anti-sexual violence orga-
    nization. In partnership with hundreds of local
    rape crisis centers, it operates the national Sexual
    Assault Hotline [(800) 656-HOPE].

Society of Children's Book Writers & Illustrators
    (SCBWI)
8271 Beverly Boulevard
Los Angeles, CA 90048
(323) 782-1010
Web site: http://www.scbwi.org
The SCBWI is a professional organization that offers
    education and information to writers and illustra-
    tors working in the field of children's literature.
    Laurie Halse Anderson is a member.

WEB SITES

Due to the changing nature of Internet links, Rosen
Publishing has developed an online list of Web
sites related to the subject of this book. This site
is updated regularly. Please use this link to access
the list:

http://www.rosenlinks.com/AAA/ander

Ambrose, Marylou. *Investigating Eating Disorders* (Anorexia, Bulimia, and Binge Eating). Berkeley Heights, NJ: Enslow Publishers, 2010.

Anderson, M. T. *The Astonishing Life of Octavian Nothing, Traitor to the Nation Vol. 1: The Pox Party.* Cambridge, MA: Candlewick Press, 2006.

Anderson, M. T. *The Astonishing Life of Octavian Nothing, Traitor to the Nation Vol. 2: The Kingdom of the Waves.* Cambridge, MA: Candlewick Press, 2008.

Bradley, Kimberly Brubaker. *Jefferson's Sons.* New York, NY: Dial Books for Young Readers, 2011.

Brown, Jennifer. *Hate List.* New York, NY: Little, Brown Books for Young Readers, 2009.

Burgan, Michael. *African Americans in the Thirteen Colonies.* New York, NY: Scholastic Children's Press, 2013.

Carosella, Melissa. *Founding Mothers: Women Who Shaped America.* Huntington Beach, CA: Teacher Created Materials, 2011.

Crawford, Brent. *Carter Finally Gets It.* New York, NY: Hyperion, 2009.

Curtis, Christopher Paul. *Elijah of Buxton.* New York, NY: Scholastic Press, 2007.

Eagen, Rachel. *Cutting and Self-Injury.* New York, NY: Crabtree Publishing, 2010.

Fletcher, Ralph. *How Writers Work: Finding a Process That Works for You.* New York, NY: HarperCollins Publishers, 2000.

Glenn, Wendy. *Laurie Halse Anderson: Speaking in Tongues.* Lanham, MD: The Scarecrow Press, 2010.

Green, John. *The Fault in Our Stars*. New York, NY:
    Dutton Books, 2012.

Hanley, Victoria. *Seize the Story*. Waco, TX: Prufrock
    Press, 2011.

Hopkins, Ellen. *Tricks*. New York, NY: Margaret K.
    McElderry Books, 2009.

Howard-Taylor, Lucy. *Biting Anorexia: A Firsthand
    Account of an Internal War*. Oakland, CA: New
    Harbinger Publications, 2009.

Jurmain, Suzanne. *The Secret of the Yellow Death:
    A True Story of Medical Sleuthing*. Boston, MA:
    Houghton Mifflin Books for Children, 2009.

Lacour, Nina. *Hold Still*. New York, NY: Dutton
    Juvenile, 2009.

Littman, Sarah Darer. *Purge*. New York, NY:
    Scholastic Press, 2009.

Majors, Kerri. *This Is Not a Writing Manual: Notes for
    the Young Writer in the Real World*. Cincinnati,
    OH: Writers Digest Books, 2013.

Mazer, Anne, and Ellen Potter. *Spilling Ink: A
    Young Writer's Handbook*. New York, NY:
    Square Fish, 2010.

Murphy, Jim. *An American Plague: The True and
    Terrifying Story of the Yellow Fever Epidemic of
    1793*. New York, NY: Clarion Books, 2003.

Nowlin, Laura. *If He Had Been With Me*. Naperville,
    IL: Sourcebooks Fire, 2013.

Palacio, R.J. *Wonder*. New York, NY: Alfred A.
    Knopf, 2012.

Paulsen, Gary. *Woods Runner*. New York, NY: Wendy
    Lamb Books, 2010.

Rainfield, Cheryl. *Scars*. Lodi, NJ: Westside Books, 2010.

Schwartz, Tina. *Writing and Publishing: The Ultimate Teen Guide*. Lanham, MD: Scarecrow Press, 2009.

Shivack, Nadia. *Inside Out: Portrait of an Eating Disorder*. New York, NY: Atheneum Books for Young Readers, 2007.

Sparks, Beatrice. *Kim: Empty Inside*. New York, NY: HarperCollins Publishers, 2010.

Stork, Fancisco. *Marcelo in the Real World*. New York, NY: Arthur A. Levine Books, 2009.

Verdi, Jessica. *My Life After Now*. Naperville, IL: Sourcebooks Fire, 2013.

Warbrick, Caroline. *Taking Action Against Eating Disorders*. New York, NY: Rosen Central, 2009.

Wilkins, Jessica. *Date Rape*. New York, NY: Crabtree Publishing, 2010.

American Library Association. "2009 Winner: Laurie Halse Anderson." Retrieved February 5, 2013 (http://www.ala.org/yalsa/booklistsawards/ bookawards/margaretaedwards/maeprevious/ edwards2009).

Anderson, Laurie Halse. "2009 Margaret A. Edwards Speech." Retrieved February 5, 2013 (http://www .ala.org/yalsa/sites/ala.org.yalsa/files/content/ booklistsawards/bookawards/margaretaedwards/ edwardsspeech.pdf).

Anderson, Laurie Halse. "Loving the Young Adult Reader Even When You Want to Strangle Him (or Her)!" *ALAN Review*, Winter 2005, pp. 53–58.

Anderson, Laurie Halse. "Mad Woman in the Forest Gets a Cottage." YouTube, November 11, 2009. Retrieved February 5, 2013 (http://www.youtube .com/watch?v=sxNkZzKmJI4).

Anderson, Laurie Halse. "Tasting the Past." *Horn Book Magazine*, March–April 2011, p. 23.

Anderson, Laurie Halse. "Triaging Rejection Pain." *Debutante Ball*, December 18, 2010. Retrieved February 5, 2013 (http://www.thedebutanteball .com/?p=13722).

Anderson, Laurie Halse. "Why Mad Woman in the Forest?" MadWomanInTheForest.com. Retrieved February 5, 2013 (http://madwomanintheforest .com/media).

AudioFile. "Laurie Halse Anderson." April–May 2009, p. 28–29.

Brown, Jennifer. "In Dreams Begin Possibilities." *Publishers Weekly*, December 20, 1999, p. 24–25.

Campbell, Sarah Stormie. "ALA...Photos." *Card Catalog of Creativity*, July 9, 2007. Retrieved February 5, 2013 (http://darkfaerielibrarian .blogspot.com/2007/07/alaphotos.html).

Florence, Debbi Michiko. "An Interview with Children's Author Laurie Halse Anderson." Retrieved February 5, 2013 (http://www .debbimichikoflorence.com/author_interviews /2002/LaurieHalseAnderson.html).

Gough, Paul. "Showtime, Lifetime Give 'Speak' Voice." *Hollywood Reporter*, July 18, 2005, pp. 1 and 7.

Hadaway, Nancy, and Terrell Young. "Good Storytelling Brings History Alive: An Interview with Laurie Halse Anderson." *Reading Today*, October–November 2012, p. 16–17.

Horning, Kathleen. "Fearless." *School Library Journal*, June 2009, p. 30–33.

Moore, Lela. "Twitter: Banned Books' New Best Friend." *New York Times*, September 28, 2010. Retrieved February 5, 2013 (http:// artsbeat.blogs.nytimes.com/2010/09/28/ twitter-banned-books-new-best-friend).

Newman, Patricia. "Who Wrote That?: Featuring Laurie Halse Anderson." *California Kids!*, March 2005. Retrieved February 5, 2013 (http://www .patriciamnewman.com/anderson.html).

Prince, Julie. "Writing from the Heart: An Interview with Laurie Halse Anderson." *Teacher Librarian*, December 2008, p. 70–71.

Reading Rockets. "A Video Interview with Laurie Halse Anderson." Retrieved February 5, 2013 (http://www.readingrockets.org/books/interviews/anderson).

Scholastic. "Biography: Laurie Halse Anderson." Retrieved February 5, 2013 (http://www.scholastic.com/teachers/contributor/laurie-halse-anderson).

Simon & Schuster. "Authors: Laurie Halse Anderson." Retrieved February 5, 2013 (http://authors.simonandschuster.com/Laurie-Halse-Anderson/1791921).

Stekley, Jolie. "SCBWI Team Blog Exclusive Interview: Laurie Halse Anderson." *Cuppa Jolie*, July 12, 2011. Retrieved February 5, 2013 (http://cuppajolie.blogspot.com/2011/07/scbwi-team-blog-exclusive-interview.html).

Teen Ink. "Author Laurie Halse Anderson." Retrieved February 5, 2013 (http://www.teenink.com/fiction/author_interviews/article/230292/Author-Laurie-Halse-Anderson).

Yahoo! Voices. "An Interview with Laurie Halse Anderson, Author of Speak." May 22, 2007. Retrieved February 5, 2013 (http://voices.yahoo.com/an-interview-laurie-halse-anderson-author-of-354501.html?cat=4).

INDEX

A

ALAN Award, 6, 74, 75
ALAN Review, 16, 22
American Library
  Association, 34, 74
*American Plague, An: The
  True and Terrifying Story
  of the Yellow Fever
  Epidemic of 1793*, 52
Anderson, Greg, 19, 43
Anderson, Laurie Halse
  advice for aspiring
    authors, 27
  childhood and education,
    10–18
  marriage and family, 19–21
  writing cottage, 70–71
  writing process, 26–27
Anderson, Meredith Lauren
  (daughter), 19, 44, 58, 64
Anderson, Stephanie
  Holcomb (daughter), 19
Antonelli, Benny
  (character), 59
Ashes, 56
AudioFile magazine, inter-
  view with, 59

B

*Big Cheese of Third
  Street, The*, 59
Blume, Judy, 35–36

C

California Kids!, interview
  with, 9, 58
Campbell, Sarah
  Stormie, 25
Card Catalog of Creativity
  (blog), 25
Catalyst, 36–38, 40, 75
Chains, 6, 53–56, 72, 74
Cook, Mattie
  (character), 50

D

*Dear Author: Letters of
  Hope*, 69
Debutante Ball, The (blog),
  post excerpts, 25
*Dirty Laundry: Stories
  About Family
  Secrets*, 66

E

Edwards, David, 15–16

F

Farrar, Straus & Giroux, 34
Fever 1793, 23, 25, 34, 46,
  48–53, 60, 75

Florence, Debbi Michiko, interview with, 16, 18, 23, 37, 40, 78
Forge, 47, 56
Franklin, Benjamin, 53

H

Hadway, Nancy, interview with, 45
Hair of Zoe Fleefenbacher Goes to School, The, 62–64
Hale, Sarah Josepha, 60–62
Halse, Frank (father) 10, 12, 14
Halse, Joyce Holcomb (mother), 10, 12, 13–14
Halse, Lisa (sister), 10
Hankins, Paul W., 35
Hannigan, Ashley (character), 38
Horning, Kathleen, interview with, 19

I

Independent Dames: What You Never Knew About the Women and Girls of the American Revolution, 62

K

Kressley, Dr. Susan J., 19, 43

L

Larrabee, Christian (stepson), 19
Larrabee, Jessica (stepdaughter), 19
Larrabee, Scot, 19, 28, 70
"Listen," 34
Love & Sex: Ten Stories of Truth, 67

M

Mad Woman in the Forest, naming of, 28
Malone, Kate (character), 36
Manlius Pebble Hill School, 14–15
Margaret A. Edwards Award, 6, 74–75
excerpts from acceptance speech, 6–7, 8, 14, 25, 34, 44
Miller, Tyler (character), 40–41
Murphy, Jim, 52

N

National Book Award, 6, 34, 72
National Coalition Against Censorship, 36
Ndito Runs, 23, 57–58
Newman, Patricia, interview with, 9, 58
No Time for Mother's Day, 58

P

"Passport," 66–67
Philadelphia Inquirer, 22
Prince, Julie, interview with, 8, 26, 30, 48
Prom, 18, 29, 38–40
Publishers Weekly, 26, 34

R

Reading Rockets, interview with, 8, 10, 11–12, 13, 22, 44, 46, 50–52, 53, 58, 59, 62, 64, 65, 77
Reading Today, interview with, 45, 46, 47

Recycle This Book: 100 Top Children's Book Authors Tell You How to Go Green, 69

S

School Library Journal, interview with, 19, 29, 30, 35, 36, 41, 43, 52–53
Scroggins, Wesley, 35, 36
Seeds of America trilogy, 53–56
Sheedy-Shea, Mrs. 12
"Snake," 67
Sordino, Melinda (character), 31–34, 35, 36, 44, 69
Speak, 6, 23–25, 26, 31–35, 36, 52, 66, 69, 72–74, 75
and censorship, 35–36
film based on, 32
Stewart, Kristen, 32

T

Teacher Librarian, interview with, 8, 26, 30, 48, 75, 78

Teen Ink, interview with, 27, 32

Thank You Sarah: The Woman Who Saved Thanksgiving, 60–62

Turkey Pox, 23, 58

Twisted, 40–41

V

Vet Volunteers series, 64–65

W

Wild at Heart series, 64–65

Wilde, Susie, interview with, 59

Wintergirls, 11, 16, 19, 41–43

Y

Young, Terrell, interview with, 45

ABOUT THE AUTHOR

Kristi Lew is the author of numerous books for young adults. Like Laurie Halse Anderson, Lew did not originally intend to become a writer. Fascinated with science from a young age, she studied biochemistry and genetics in college. After working in genetics laboratories and teaching high school science for about a decade, Lew finally discovered her true passion. When she is not writing, she can often be found with her nose in a book.

PHOTO CREDITS

Cover, pp. 3, 7, 11, 13 Courtesy of Laurie Halse Anderson; pp. 14–15 Manlius Pebble Hill School; p. 17 Aimin Tang/E+/Getty Images; pp. 20–21 © Syracuse Newspapers/D Lassman/The Image Works; pp. 24, 60–61, 73 Simon & Schuster; p. 27 © Syracuse Newspapers/S Dunn/The Image Works; p. 28 Doug Lemke/Shutterstock.com; pp. 32–33 Showtime/Photofest; pp. 38–39 © Syracuse Newspapers/G Walts/The Image Works; p. 42 Monkey Business Images/Shutterstock.com; p. 45 © Syracuse Newspapers/J Talbot/The Image Works; pp. 48–49 MPI/Archive Photos/Getty Images; pp. 50–51 © Syracuse Newspapers/P Chen/The Image Works; pp. 54–55 Library of Congress Prints and Photographs Division; p. 60 Hulton Archive/Getty Images; p. 63 Stock Montage/Archive Photos/Getty Images; p. 68 © AP Images; pp. © 70–71 Syracuse Newspapers/J Berry/The Image Works; pp. 76–77 Anthony Pidgeon/Redferns/Getty Images; cover and interior pages background (marbleized texture) javarman/Shutterstock.com; cover and interior pages (book) www.iStockphoto.com/Andrzej Tokarski; interior pages background (ice surface) © iStockphoto.com/dmax-foto.

Designer: Nicole Russo; Editor: Kathy Kuhtz Campbell;
Photo Researcher: Marty Levick